Punch Needle for Beginners

Table of Contents

Introduction

Crafting at home is becoming something the cool kids do. In searching for inexpensive and worthwhile things to do, or creative ways to make extra cash, many people are turning to the past and the crafting arts of earlier ages. In particular, one of the first types of crafting many people start with is punch needle embroidery. Part of its popularity is due to how easy it is. All that is required is a special needle, yarn, and some loosely weaved fabric. You use the needle to push the yarn through the fabric. Obviously, it's not quite that simple, but the basic technique is not much more complex. There aren't any fancy knots or elaborate stitches. You don't even really need to count stitches, as most punch needle embroidery will form a picture, sort of like a painting, so keeping track of what you're doing is fairly straightforward. In fact, it was sometimes called 'punch painting' at points in its history.

Completed punch needle projects are incredibly versatile, as well. Many can simply stand on their own, becoming a painting or even being framed. Others with a sturdier construction can be made into rugs, which is a traditional use for punch needle embroidery. Punch needle projects can be used to make clothes a little more attractive, turned into ornaments, or even made into 3D art. Crafters, the creative bunch that they are, are always finding new uses for their completed punch needle projects.

There are a number of variations, called variously Punch, Punch Embroidery, Punch Needle Embroidery, Russian Embroidery, and Bunka. These different types have very distinct styles that are associated with them. For example, Russian embroidery usually features geometric patterns in red, which was thought to be the color of beauty in medieval Russia. Bunka, a Japanese style of punch embroidery, is often mistaken for actual oil painting, as it features fine detailed and complex colors.

History of Punch Needle Embroidery

Just those few examples reveal the rich and varied history of punch needle embroidery. As an art form, it's been around since at least the European Middle Ages, and perhaps as far back as ancient Egypt. Its origins are not clear, but we can say with certainty that it has been practiced by all levels of society, and by both men and women. Like crochet and knitting, for example, punch needle embroidery was popular with sailors at sea. Experts in knots and rope, these crafts were useful and provided a way to keep busy on long voyages between ports.

In Russia, punch needle embroidery was historically associated with a religious minority. After a change in the Russian Orthodox Church, punch needle embroidery became associated with dissenters from those new changes. Called 'Old Believers,' much of their religious clothing was decorated with the red, geometric variety of punch needle embroidery that is now called Russian punch embroidery. Patterns of shapes and combinations of colors in Russian embroidery are so specific to different ethnicities that an expert can use the pattern to identify where a particular piece of embroidery came from.

Bunka shishu, frequently shortened to bunka, is a Japanese style of punch needle embroidery that uses silk (or rayon in the last half-century or so) instead of yarn. The thinner thread allows for more detailed work, mimicking the finer point of a paintbrush.

Today, punch needle embroidery is experiencing a revival as crafting, in general, becomes more popular. With modern attention has come modern takes on this traditional practice. Artists working to create contemporary punch needleworks have paved the way for home hobbyists to express themselves. Now, you can find patterns for any of the traditional styles, or contemporary styles expressed through punch needle embroidery, or even a blending of the traditional and the modern.

What To Expect

This book will provide a complete introduction to the art of punch needle embroidery. Before you even start with your first project, you will have an understanding of the basic terminology and the materials you'll need to get started. Each step along the way will be covered in detail, with multiple methods covered for things like transferring patterns and preparing your embroidery hoop. The technique of how to create punch needle embroidery will also be outlined, with some tips to make things easier for beginners.

Once you're ready to start, you'll find a range of punch needle projects that you can try. It is recommended that beginners start at the first project and work their way back, as different techniques are discussed in different projects. The difficulty level rises also, though all of the projects are at the beginner level. At the end of each one, you'll have a fun new piece of decor or useful household item.

Far more than just using a punch needle on a kit that all came together from a craft store, you'll learn how to put your individual stamp on your projects. A couple of different methods of creating your own frames are outlined, so you can truly customize your projects. You'll even find instructions for making your own, custom punch needle.

By the end of the book, you'll be able to move on to intermediate or even expert level punch needle projects. You'll also have tried creating a few of your own designs and learned ways to customize your punch needle embroidery to you.

As you work through the projects, take your time, and don't rush. And most of all, have fun!

Chapter One:
Supplies

Punch needle embroidery only needs a few basic supplies. If you've got some experience with other crafts, you may already have some of this stuff around. Even if you're starting from scratch, putting together the basics shouldn't cost too much. It's easy to find punch needle kits for beginners, which will have the basics all together for you. The cheapest kits are only as expensive as a couple of cups of fancy coffee. Putting together your own supplies may be even cheaper if you have a sharp eye for a deal.

There are some more expensive variations on the basics. There are a few slightly different designs of punch needle, which you may want to try out before you settle on your favorite. Yarn can be another good place to splurge, as different weights and qualities of yarn can provide different effects for your project. Some weights and types of yarn may also be easier to use than others.

As your confidence level grows and you become more comfortable with punch needle crafting, you may want to try variations on some of these basics. Switching out embroidery silk for yarn might provide more control and look more refined, instead of the folk-rustic look usually associated with punch needle embroidery. Different styles of punch needle embroidery may also require different materials. For example, the Japanese style bunka works specifically with silk or rayon. Working with silk comes with its own set of challenges; however, that will be covered only briefly in this beginners' book.

For most of the projects in these pages, the cheap and basic should be all you need. As a beginner, you won't need much, or any, of the fancier options explained here. However, detailing some of the fancier options can help give you an idea of some of the more creative possibilities of punch needle embroidery. A bit of a background in the terms used can also be helpful if you're going to do some further reading or explanation, so you understand what everyone is talking about. Don't worry about getting lost in advanced stuff, though, as the basic supplies will be reviewed again before you punch your first stitch. In the meantime, let's start with the star of the show.

Punch Needle

You can't really do punch needle embroidery without the punch needle. The tool itself was introduced in the 1890s. Prior to that, the hook (something like a crochet hook) for making rugs sort of did the same thing, only backward, pulling the yarn through the fabric rather than punching it.

All punch needles share some fundamental attributes. The grip was traditionally wooden, but today it might also be plastic or metal. Different needles have different grip designs, which you may want to sample so you can find one that fits most comfortably in your hand. At the business end is the stainless steel needle. It's hollow (like the whole thing), with a hole near the sharp end. The length of the needle determines the depth of the loop that is being punched. The needle pushes through until the fabric runs up against the stop when the fabric runs up against the grip. Thicker needles may be longer and thinner needles shorter, though different mixes are available. There are also punch needles that have adjustable lengths, such as the ultrapunch. Three most preferred punch needles are the Oxford Punch needle, height adjustable punch needle, and the ultra punch needle.

In general, a larger diameter needle can allow you to use a thicker, tougher yarn for your project, for example, if you were making a rug. That's going to be harder to push through, however. Thinner needles are easier to punch through, but only allow for narrow yarns. There are also mini-needles that are used with finer yarn or embroidery floss, and are used to create finer projects with tighter stitching.

The punch needle is hollow so the yarn can be run through it. Threading it can be a pain, though most come with a special threading tool. One variety in particular, the Oxford punch needle, has a channel down the side, which makes threading the needle much easier.

Yarn

It's the same stuff that knitters use for their projects, and if you're an experienced knitter, you may already have a good handle on the subject. Many knitters can be fairly particular about the yarn they use, perhaps because a low-quality yarn can make a sweater or hat scratchy and uncomfortable. With punch needle embroidery, that's less of an issue. Even when punch needle embroidery is used to decorate clothing, it's not going to irritate the wearer. There's no need to break the bank paying for first-rate yarn with punch needle embroidery.

A lot could be said about yarn, the different terms used in discussing it, the materials it's made from, its source, etc. The list could go on for a while. It's a topic that could fill a whole book on its own, and you don't actually need to know the great majority of it to get started with punch needle embroidery. Even the cheapest yarn can be used to make a beautiful punch needle project. A bit of a grounding in the subject is important, however. The terms you are most likely to encounter in the context of yarn types are "ply," "hank," "skein," "donut," and "cakes." However, as a beginner, it's fine to just choose a yarn that suits the color and thickness you'd prefer for a specific project.

Different thicknesses of yarn can be used. Using a different weight of yarn can give different effects in the finished project, and some projects (perhaps best saved for when you're comfortable with the basics) use both thicker and thinner yarns. The other thing to keep in mind with yarn thickness, however, is how well it stays put. Because punch needle embroidery is, essentially, just pushing a loop of yarn through the foundation fabric so that the material pinches it in place. If the yarn is too slippery or too thin, it can be easily pulled out of the foundation fabric, or even just fall out. The other side of this equation is the thread count of the foundation fabric. A higher thread count fabric will be a tighter weave and be better able to hold thinner weights of yarn, or even silk. Lower thread count foundation fabric should be used with a thicker weight of yarn.

Yarn weights start at 0 and go up to 7, with 0 being lace-fine and 7 being jumbo thick. The lightest weight yarns (0, 1, 2) are the finest and are difficult to find. Size 3 is light and size 4 is medium. Go for size 4 when starting out with your first few projects. Size 5 and 6 are bulky and super-bulky respectively. They are also not usually used for punch needle embroidery, so you don't need to worry about them. Most other types of yarn will work. Using different thicknesses of yarn, or yarn made from sheep, bamboo, or something else, should all work without a problem.

One other variety of wool to be aware of is rug wool yarn, which is different from the stuff used for knitting. Rug yarn has a rougher texture and is more resistant to wear. As you might have guessed, rug yarn is specifically for making rugs if that's something you want to try. Otherwise, it's not something to worry about. Another variety, felting yarn, is usually what you'll find in hobby stores listed as 100% wool. Felting yarn is a single ply, meaning it's only a single strand. This is in contrast to normal yarn, which is usually several strands twisted together. It will work fine for punch needle embroidery.

One traditional and interesting idea is to use strips of wool fabric rather than yarn. It can be a way to save money if you're willing to put in the foot work. Historically, the strips of wool fabric used were taken from old clothes and rags, reusing the fabric rather than disposing of it. Following in our forebears' footsteps, you can also reuse old clothes in your punch needle projects. In particular, you can find wool clothes at second-hand or thrift shops. You can take out the buttons, zipper, and other extra bits, then cut the fabric into narrow strips. The traditional width for these strips is 1.4 inch, and might be a good place to start. It offers a balance between fineness, 1/4 inch being narrow enough to be useful in punch needle embroidery, but not so narrow that it's fiddly and difficult to cut.

Other options include buttonhole thread, which is a thicker variety of (usually silk) thread. As you may have guessed, it's used for sewing on buttons, but the fact that it's thicker makes it a decent option for punch needle embroidery. Silk embroidery floss is also commonly used.

Foundation Fabric

The foundation fabric is the cloth that is tightly stretched across the embroidery frame and which you punch the yarn through. A special type of fabric isn't necessarily required. Technically, any woven fabric might work, though some are definitely going to be a lot easier. As a beginner who is just learning the ropes, you'll want to stick to one of a few different options, which are detailed below. Generally, the foundation fabric should be about 50% cotton and 50% polyester and should be tightly woven. They should be slightly stiff and hold the yarn loop even after the embroidery ring has been removed. Most of them are going to be available in white or off-white, though if you look, you can certainly find other background colors. Also, be aware that because of the stiffness, tightness of the weave, and all the rest, they are likely to fray.

The best options for foundation fabrics include:

<u>Monk's cloth</u> - One of the two most common punch needle foundation fabrics. Monk's cloth has a simple over-under weave that is easy to work with when using a punch needle. Some craft stores carry Monk's cloth that might have other uses, leading it to have a tighter weave that won't work as well with punch needle embroidery. You're looking for monk's cloth that is 14 or 15 count, meaning it has 14 or 15 threads per inch. Mistakes are also easy to fix when using monk's cloth. You can pull the less-than-perfect stitches and, thanks to the fabric's characteristic

weave, even out the threads so that you can punch into the same spot on the material without a problem. It will probably work best with yarn, particularly of weight 4 or 5.

Weaver's cloth - This is the other most common choice for foundation fabric. You'll find it in many beginners' kits because it's a good choice for finer projects using thinner yarn. It can be used with thinner yarn, or with other options like buttonhole thread or embroidery floss. Thicker yarn, and the thicker needle you'll need for it, will be hard to push through the weaver's cloth. *Aida cloth* is similar, used most commonly for cross-stitch, and can be used for a lot of the same projects.

Denim - Everyone has some denim in their closet. In addition to making hard-wearing pants, it can also serve as a foundation cloth, making jeans a good candidate for a little embroidered decoration. You can find different weights of denim at your local fabric or hobby store without much problem. A denim blend with stretch polyester should not be used. Heavy denim works better than lighter weight fabric, as it will hold on to the loops more tightly.

Linen - A truly fancy option for foundation cloth. It tends to be more expensive, but also is the most versatile, being sturdy while not being too rough. Depending on the linen, it might be difficult to keep the loops from slipping out, so it might be good to save this for some more advanced projects.

In addition to these, there are a number of other possible candidates for foundation fabric. Most of these offer additional variety or are useful for special projects. For example, denim, burlap, and linen are available in a variety of colors if you need a particular shade. You might work on denim if you're decorating clothes. For a beginners' project, however, it's best to start with monk's or aida cloth, or weaver's cloth if you're working with thinner yarn. They're going to be the easiest to work with and least frustrating.

Embroidery Frame

The frame or ring is used to hold the foundation fabric tight, spreading the weave open to make it easier to punch through, and also to hold the work in place. The standard, traditional embroidery hoop is actually two separate hoops, one small enough to fit just inside the other. The larger, outer hoop has a small threaded closure that can be used to tighten the hoop down. Most kits come with a version of this basic hoop. These wooden hoops, when bought on their own, are just a couple of dollars. Some slightly more expensive wooden hoops are more appealing aesthetically, with finer wood or fancier closures. These are meant to be used for projects such as hangings when a punch needle project is going to be left in the hoop for display.

We'll go over how to set up the frame with the foundation fabric in the next chapter, along with a few tips to make that easier. However, be aware that the basic wooden hoops are generally the most difficult to set up. The foundation fabric is also more likely to slip in the middle of the project, so that you'll have to stop, center the pattern, and tighten everything over again. There are a few ways to make them easier to work with.

Another option is to get a plastic embroidery hoop. Obviously, these look a little less attractive, and you're not going to want to leave the embroidery in a plastic hoop to display it. But plastic hoops are much easier to set up and also are much better at keeping the foundation fabric tight. The inner and outer hoops interlock, providing more friction and keeping the fabric in place. Plastic hoops are going to be the best choice when the embroidery is going to be taken out of the hoop and used in some other sort of project. Plastic hoops are slightly more expensive, but can be used many times.

Not all frames are hoops, though that is most common for hobbyists. It's possible to make your own frames pretty easily without much carpentry skill, or none at all. It's possible to make them yourself without too much carpentry skill. Another option could be artist canvases, which are already in a square frame if that's what you're looking for. Some punch needle artists have found artists' canvas too difficult to use, however.

Finally, there are large, rectangular gripping frames. These use either strips of carpet tacks or plastic to hold the fabric tightly in place. These can be great as the fabric will genuinely stay very tight. However, they are usually over a foot in size and are more commonly used to make rugs or wall hangings, or other large projects.

Crafting Supplies

All of the usual subjects are going to get a work out here. Scissors are a good idea, of course, for trimming thread and cutting the foundation fabric. With fabric scissors, sharper is always better, as sharper scissors will cut a cleaner edge with less fraying and less effort. A water-erasable marker or pencil can be helpful, particularly if you're going to use them to trace the pattern onto the foundation cloth. There are a few ways to transfer the patterns, a few of which will be covered in the next chapter.

Adhesive can also be a good idea. If you're leaving your punch needle project on the hoop, you might go so far as to glue the tightened foundation fabric onto the hoop, so it stays tight. The method for doing that will be explained below. If your punch needle embroidery is going to experience any wear, for example, if you made a rug or are embellishing clothes, use adhesive on the flat stitch side of the embroidery. It'll just make sure everything stays in place. A pair of pliers and a screwdriver can also be helpful when trying to get your embroidery hoop to fasten closed and stay tight.

Patterns

The outline of your project. You may have a pattern in mind, or you may get one from a kit. There are any number of free patterns out there, enough to keep a punch needle enthusiast happy for a long time. If you're looking for more challenging or fancier projects, you can also buy patterns online or elsewhere.

The great majority of patterns you find on the internet are going to fall into the traditional styles of punch needle embroidery. The rustic American aesthetic is the most common out there. It's possible to find patterns that are designed in a whole range of styles, however, though some may take some digging. There is a thriving community of punch needlers creating gaming or genre-related patterns.

Punch needle embroidery is sometimes called 'punch needle painting,' and like painting, you don't necessarily need a pattern. Like an artist at a canvas, you can just start creating.

Chapter Two: Getting Started

You've got your punch needle, foundation fabric, and all the rest of it, and are ready to begin. Before you start poking your needle into things, though, there are a couple more things to deal with. The foundation fabric has to be stretched across the embroidery hoop and be secured, the pattern has to be transferred, and your needle has to be threaded. All of those steps, with tips to make them a bit easier, will be laid out for you. Punch needle embroidery *is* pretty simple, but there is a little bit of basic technique to review.

Before doing anything else, make sure you've got all the supplies needed for the whole project. That includes all of the stuff listed in Chapter One, plus whatever else you might need for your project. As you'll see when working through some of the projects in this book, punch needle embroidery can be used in a whole range of ways to add color and beauty to many aspects of your life. This chapter explains how to prepare your fabric, thread your punch needle, and set up the punch needle hoop. The next chapter teaches you how to needle punch any pattern. So, let's get started!

Set Up

The steps outlined here should work for just about any punch needle embroidery project. Preparing your project has stages, and some steps can be done more than one way, so it might seem like the preparations are complicated and time-consuming. In reality, most of these things shouldn't take very long. After practicing on a project or two, it'll be a snap to get everything ready.

1. *Preshrink Foundation Fabric*

    Just about all of the foundation fabric options are either natural fiber or a blend. It should therefore be washed and dried to shrink the fabric before it's used in any project. All it should take is throwing it in the washing machine and then the dryer, and it can save you a headache later.

2. *Transfer the Pattern*

    Transferring patterns can take some fiddling, and it's a part of the process that many people don't enjoy. Punch needle patterns don't have any of the more complex markings of a sewing pattern, which makes them less frustrating to work with. As with many things, the right tools help to make things easier. Three different methods are going to be described,

It is possible to buy foundation fabric with the pattern already drawn out on it. Some kits may provide that, or there are a number of small companies catering to punch needlers that provide them. You should be able to find a great range of options on Etsy.com, or similar sites.

The first method requires a lightbox or a window and a sunny day. Pin the pattern to the wrong side of the foundation fabric, which is the side that will not be displayed. Make sure that both the fabric and pattern are flat and without any wrinkles. Place the foundation fabric with the pattern behind, on a lightbox or against a window with the sun behind it, right side of the foundation fabric facing you. The pattern should show through and can be traced with a pencil or erasable marker.

The second method uses fabric carbon paper. If you're old enough to remember making copies in school with carbon paper, you'll have some idea how it works. Be sure to get carbon paper specifically for use with fabric, though. Place the foundation fabric on a flat surface, right side up. Place the carbon paper face down on the foundation fabric. The pattern goes on top. Pin everything together so it doesn't move. Use something stiff with a fine point to trace the lines of the pattern, pressing firmly. The pressure transfers carbon to the foundation fabric where you traced the lines. Carbon paper might be a little harder to find, although you can probably find some online. Different colors of carbon paper are also available, so try to find something that contrasts with the color of the foundation fabric to make things easier.

The third method is a little more involved, but it will work even if you don't have a carbon paper, a lightbox, or the sun isn't being cooperative that day. You will need some chalk dust or carbon powder. Use a needle to poke holes along the lines of the pattern, focusing on corners and details. Lay out and pin the pattern to the foundation fabric. Brush the pattern with the powder so that the foundation fabric is marked. Remove the pattern and connect the chalk dots. You can poke the holes after lining up and pinning the pattern to the foundation fabric, although you are also likely to poke holes through the foundation fabric, which you may want to avoid.

Many creative people have found ways to transfer patterns to paper. If you're artistic enough, you could even transfer the pattern freehand. These are just a few basic ways to do it. If you have a project that presents an unusual problem, check the internet to see if others have found tricks to make things easier.

3. *Stretching the Foundation Fabric in the Embroidery Hoop*

This is a crucial step. Keeping the foundation fabric tight in the hoop is going to make everything easier, so it's worth it to spend a few moments doing it well. The more tightly stretched the foundation fabric is, the easier it will be to push the needle through the weave, and the less effort each stitch will take. Since even a small project can need dozens of stitches, the difference between tight and not quite tight enough is important. On the other hand, stretching the fabric too tightly will lead it to 'spring' back together once removed from the hoop, so that the foundation fabric ends up being puckered together. Finding the middle-ground will be easy with a little practice.

One tip that will help keep the fabric from slipping in the hoop is to wrap the inner hoop with a bias band or a strip of cloth. Wrap it completely so that no wood is showing. The foundation fabric is then placed across the inner hoop; then the outer hoop is tightened on the outside. Tighten the outer hoop so that the foundation fabric is held, but not too tightly. Pull the foundation fabric more tightly, going around the outside of the hoop, until it is as tight as you can get it. Tighten the outside hoop as much as you can.

If you're not planning on taking the project out of the hoop, you can take it a step further and glue the foundation cloth into the hoop. Simply cut the foundation fabric around the outside of the hoop, leaving a bit of a fringe. Fold this inside the hoop and glue it down. The fabric folded inside should be glued to the hoop, and should not be long enough to overlap the fabric you're working.

4. *Threading the Punch Needle*

Threading needles is frequently frustrating, and sometimes punch needles have a reputation for being hard to thread. The punch needle and handle is hollow, so that the yarn has to be pushed through the whole way. Most punch needles these days come with a special tool to help thread it, though, making the process much easier.

Chapter Three: Start Needle Punching

In the last chapter, you set up your fabric, punch needle, and frame. Once you have everything prepped, you can go straight into producing your first piece of punch needle embroidery. But, before you begin, make sure you're using the right technique.

Basic Needle Punching Technique

There is a little bit more to it than simply punching the needle through the fabric, though not too much more. The punch needle itself needs to be used in a specific way to get the best result. There are also a few rules on how to arrange stitches and loops, which will also improve your odds of an attractive finished product.

Setup Your Yarn so it Unwinds Smoothly. - The first rule to follow when setting up is that you don't want any tension on the yarn as you're placing stitches. Tension on the yarn can cause uneven loop sizes, loose stitches, stitches pulling out, and a range of other problems. Make sure your yarn can unwind easily.

Position your Punch Needle and Punch - Place the needle point on one of the lines of the pattern. To use the needle, position it so that the opening of the needle is facing in the direction you are punching. The needle should be as close to a right angle to the foundation fabric as it can be. Push the needle all the way in, until the stop runs up against the foundation fabric. Pull the end of the yarn through to the far side. The side of the fabric facing you is technically the 'wrong side,' the side not traditionally meant to be seen. Since this technique was originally used with rugs, the 'right side,' the side facing away from you, is going to be the one with the longer loops, while the side facing you is going to have flat stitches. Obviously, you're not limited to rugs, and you can display whichever side you want, as many people find the flat stitch side more attractive.

Pull your Needle Back to Make Loops - Withdraw the needle, but only just, being sure not to lift it too far. Move the needle over slightly, and punch through the foundation fabric again. The stitches should be about as far apart as the diameter of the yarn. For example, if you were to use a ¼ inch strip of wool fabric, you want the stitches to be about ¼ inch apart. On the other hand, try not to have the stitches much closer than that, as the foundation fabric will tend to bunch up. Again, be sure to push the needle all the way through. Otherwise, the loops will be of uneven size.

Outline the Pattern and Start Filling In - As you continue filling in the pattern, follow the outline of the shape and begin spiraling into the center, making sure you're covering the foundation cloth, so there aren't any patches. Stagger the stitches so that they don't line up, as the finished product might look a little odd otherwise. Also, lining stitches up too closely might actually weaken the foundation fabric itself. As you add stitches, angle the needle very slightly away from existing stitches so that the loops and stitches aren't tangled.

Trim Loose Ends- Once you've completed a section or a whole project, flip over to the loopy, right side. Take a moment to trim off loose ends. You may notice the outline of the shapes on the right side are indistinct, with loops not being placed quite correctly. It's possible to take the point of your needle, or other thin tool, and poke the loops into the right spots and clean up the pattern's outline. You may also see that, as you add more stitches to complete the pattern, shapes begin to become defined. That's only if you're interested in displaying the loop side, however. If you prefer the flat stitch side, it shouldn't take much more work to be made presentable.

Finish your Project - Once you've reached the end of a section or project, you can just trim off the yarn. There are no knots needed to keep everything in place, as it's all being held by the foundation fabric already.

That doesn't necessarily have to be the end of the project, as punch needle embroidery can be used in many different ways. If you're planning on leaving your finished embroidery in the hoop, there are still a few steps you can take, if you like. You'll probably want to cut off the excess foundation fabric; the remainder of which can be glued down as has already been covered. Another option is to fold over the excess foundation fabric and run a stitch through it to keep it hidden behind. Either way, another piece of cloth or a backing material can be cut to shape and either glued or sewn onto the open back of the embroidery hoop.

Otherwise, you can remove the foundation cloth from the embroidery hoop to prepare for the next step in the project. The project should be fairly stable once it's out of the hoop, so you don't need to treat it too gently. You can even machine wash most punch needle projects, although be sure to check to see if your materials are colorfast.

Learning the basic technique and setting up the materials is just the first part, the hard work you have to do before you get to the fun part! Crafting is all about unleashing the creative part of your personality and enjoying the art, so the rest of the book consists of patterns and instructions for projects you can do yourself.

They are all beginner-level projects, with simple patterns and easy to follow instructions. Even though they are easy, they are all fun and attractive. At the end of all of them, you'll have a beautiful crafting project you'll be happy to display in your home.

Chapter Four:
Hanging Art on the Wall

Any punch needle project has two major parts. The first is the punch needle embroidery itself, 'punch painting' the image with yarn. The second part is what you do with the embroidery once it is complete, whether it is to simply display it, or to turn it into a pillow, or even decorate clothing. They're both fun in their own ways, but often require different tools and materials. To keep things easy and help with your organization, those two parts are going to be separated and covered individually. That means you can get everything together for the punch needle embroidery and finish that completely before having to worry about getting everything together for part two, finishing your crafting project to display.

The first project is a very simple one that is going to end up where art traditionally is displayed, hanging on the wall. Punch needle embroidery can be beautiful just displayed as it is, still in the embroidery hoop. The image is also a fairly simple one, offering plenty of opportunities to practice your stitches. But, if you want to add a few embellishments, it is possible to take this beginner's pattern and add some more detail. Before we get into anything fancy, however, let's make sure the basics are covered.

First, make sure you have all of your materials. You will need:

- A punch needle (and threading tool)

- Foundation cloth (monk's cloth or weaver's cloth are best)

- Yarn, at least 3 colors

- Embroidery hoop

- Pattern - found on the next page

- Washable fabric marker or other marking tool

- Scissors

- Bias band or other strips of thin cloth (optional)

- Glue (optional).

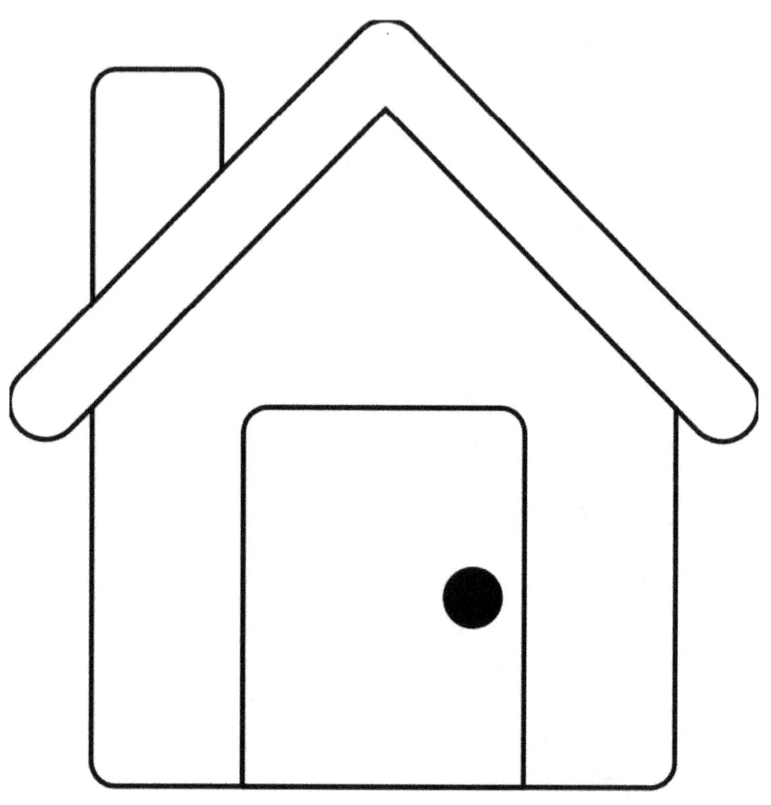

Step One: Transfer the Pattern

Once you've collected all your materials for the punch needle embroidery, you can get started. The first step of any punch needle embroidery project is to transfer your pattern to your foundation fabric. You can flip back to Chapter One to check out some detailed strategies for making that easy. As a quick review, though, we'll touch on some of the key points. First off, you'll want to print out the pattern you find in this book. Then you can use a lightbox and a fabric marker to trace the pattern onto the fabric. Another option is to use carbon paper or poke holes and use chalk powder.

This pattern is obviously quite simple, but it will still make an attractive project. Alternatively, this can be your first opportunity to add your own style to your project, with this pattern serving as an outline to give you a chance to try out different ways of elaborating on the basics. You can add a window or a flower to the pattern and copy it over to the foundation fabric, or add as much or as little as you like. Once you gain a little confidence, you can also add elements as you're punching yarn. Punch needle embroidery is known as 'punch painting' because it is so similar to placing paint on a canvas, and in the same way, yarn stitches can be added or shaped without a pattern if you have a clear idea of what you're trying to add. Also, remember that if you don't like something you've done, it can be undone very easily and without ruining the overall project. Punch needle embroidery is a very forgiving craft.

Step Two: Prepare Embroidery Hoop

It will help, as you work on future punch needle projects, if you can have some idea of how you're going to use a particular piece of embroidery. In this case, the punch needle embroidery is going to be displayed as a hanging, so that you can leave the fabric in the hoop. If that's your plan, you might want to invest in a reasonably nice wooden hoop. It can be helpful to wrap the smaller, inside hoop in a bias band or strips of fabric. Doing so will make the fit between the hoops a little tighter, creating more friction and, therefore, a tighter hold on the foundation fabric.

Another good option that will make sure the foundation fabric is secured is to glue it to the hoop. The method for doing that was described briefly in the previous chapter. Just be aware that gluing the foundation fabric down is a fairly conclusive step that is difficult to undo. Also, keep in mind that traditionally, the flat stitch side of the embroidery is the wrong side, the side that's not visible. If you want to glue the fabric in to display the flat stitches, flip the hoop around, so you're punching into the front.

If you're planning on moving it to another frame, you may want to use a plastic hoop, as the fabric is less likely to shift as you're working on it without needing to use other tricks. Just be sure to get the foundation fabric as tight as possible.

Step Three: Preparing the Punch Needle

You're actually going to need to do this a few times throughout a project. With this first, basic project, you're going to be using at least three colors of yarn, and therefore going to need to thread the punch needle at least three times. Keep in mind that each stitch is separate; you can switch colors between stitches without any problems or worrying yourself that the stitches will come out.

Most punch needles come with a threading tool. This tool is a simple loop of thin wire that can be threaded through the punch needle. The yarn is put through the loop and is drawn with it back through the hollow punch needle.

If you lose your threading tool or if your punch needle didn't come with one, don't worry. Any length of thin wire, preferably one that's a little stiff, will work. Even a length of thread will work in a pinch. You'll also need to thread the yarn through the small hole in the point of the needle, so that the loose end of the thread is behind and below the punch needle.

Before you start, remember that any tension in the yarn can lead to odd size loops or disappearing stitches. Do your best to keep your yarn loose and flowing freely.

Step Four: Start Punching

Remember that the side with the loops is the side that was traditionally displayed, so a traditional piece of punch needle embroidery will be punched from inside the hoop. If you want to display the flat stitches, you can turn the hoop around and punch from the 'visible' side. Flipping the hoop around shouldn't change anything about how to make the stitches.

Orient the needle so that the open side is facing in the direction you're punching, in the direction you move between punches. Make sure it's also at approximately right angles to the foundation fabric. Using a 90-degree angle makes it more likely the needle will slide easily through the fabric. Push firmly through. When the foundation fabric is stretched, it shouldn't take too much effort to push the needle through the weave.

Don't hold onto the yarn; just push the needle through and let the yarn run. Be sure to push all the way down to the stop so that you're forming even-sized loops.

The house picture is made up of four parts, including the door, the house front, the roof, and the chimney. Each shape should be outlined and punched individually. For example, you'd want to punch the outline of the door and then continue in a spiral around until the whole door is filled. Then, start outlining the house front, spiraling in until the house front is full. Repeat for the roof and the chimney. Remember that you want to stagger the stitches so that the holes don't line up in straight lines. Use black yarn to fill in the doorknob.

That's it for the hard part! You've completed the punching part of your punch needle project. If you're planning on displaying the looped side of the piece, you can take your punch needle and arrange the loops neatly.

At this point, you could call the project complete. In particular, if you've already trimmed the edges of the foundation fabric and glued them back, it will already be a neat little piece. However, even in that case, there's a little more that you can do. With some felt fabric and a little patience, you can finish up the back so that it has a finished, attractive look from every angle. For the moment, though, this is an opportunity to take a break or put the project aside to pick up later.

Step Five: Finish with Style

This is where the second part of the project begins, taking your piece of embroidery and bringing it to a finished state that you're proud to display. It really doesn't take much to give it a polished look. You'll need to get:

- A needle

- Thread (preferably that matches the color of the foundation fabric)

- Felt fabric

- Scissors

If you haven't trimmed the back, now is a good opportunity. You'll still want to trim off some of the excess foundation fabric, but you'll still want to leave a little loose. Take a needle and thread, fold the remainder of the foundation fabric behind and put a running stitch through the fabric to itself to keep it back. Next, lay out the felt fabric. Put the embroidery hoop down on the fabric. Mark and cut out a circle that is a little larger than the embroidery hoop. The overlapping felt can be folded below to give the felt backing a clean edge. Using a needle and thread, sew the round felt to the back of the punch needle project, into the foundation fabric at the back of the hoop. Wire can be attached to the back of the hoop so it can be hung.

Congratulations! You've completed your first punch needle project.

Chapter Five:
Easy Plant Patterns

You are through with your very first project. The last chapter included quite a bit of detail on transferring your pattern, preparing your embroidery hoop and punch needle, needle punching, and finally, finishing your artwork.

The materials you will need for the following try-yourself projects are much the same, except that you will want to pull out lots of colors of yarn to do your trial-and-error this time. A quick list of the supplies needed is included below:

- Punch needles (keep your regular and thin punch needle handy).

- Selection of foundation fabrics (choose between three different types of foundation fabrics such as monk's cloth, linen, and weaver's cloth).

- Yarn (10-15 colors of your choice).

- Embroidery hoops (wooden and plastic).

- Washable marker and pencil.

The projects described here are intended to help you get familiar with the different materials used for needle punching projects. You want to try out how yarns match up with different types of fabrics. You also want to draw freehand and craft your first few designs, fixing the cloth on wooden and plastic hoops to see the type of stretch they provide to those fabrics. These precise activities will give the practical exposure you need to play around with the different materials, punch needle tools, frames, and yarns. You want to pick up the basic hints here and experiment with the look and feel that you prefer.

Step One: Transfer Your Pattern

This time, you want to draw simple plant designs to start testing all those wonderful ideas. Plant patterns are great starting points as they teach you the lines and curves you need for most projects covered in the other chapters. Here are three simple patterns you want to use on a foundation fabric:

Plant in a pot set up on a table - Draw a small rectangular table with a pot over it, and then draw the stem with four or five equally spaced leaves. Make sure you have at least three colors here: one for the table, another for the stem, and the third color for the leaves. You may even choose different shades for the leaves and the stem.

Plant Pattern – Use your creative imagination to draw a stem (think of shrubs, tall plants, herbs, or even trees) and then add leaves with shapes and sizes you think will match well with the stem. You want at least two colors of yarn here, but it's perfectly fine to go with many more colors if you want to display shades of just green, or maybe shades of autumn.

Flower with Petal Pattern – This one makes a color-rich design. Draw a flower and surround it with leaves. This pattern gives you maximum flexibility to create different shapes for petals and leaves. You can even go for a bunch of flowers in the middle of the pattern, possibly with different shapes for petals, and then add many different types of leaves. This design makes it possible to combine different shades of yarn and test out regular and thin punch needles to get a feel of the types of loops your chosen needle punching material will create on fabric.

Step Two: Prepare the Embroidery Hoop

This is a flexible and simple step. Choose a different frame each time and a different fabric, too, to stretch it across and start punching. Remember that this activity is more of a fun project, and you don't want to think too much about things going wrong. In the end, experimenting with materials will help you learn from your mistakes. However, you want to be sure you have incorporated advice on the basic aspects of needle punching materials discussed so far.

Step Three: Prepare the Punch Needle

Thread the punch needle you chose to match the fabric. This step requires you to apply the understanding you acquired in the previous chapters.

Choose a punch needle that fits in the weave of your chosen fabric. You have relatively less flexibility here. If you choose a thin weave, you want to go for the ultra punch needle and not the regular one so that the needle does not tear through the weaving.

Step Four: Start Punching

It's time to see how your project turns out. Start punching your designs, one after the other, making sure you apply the basic technique covered in the previous chapter. You want to try this with a friend to finish off your three patterns faster and also compare results later on. By the end of the three projects, you would have acquired a basic level of expertise in choosing fabrics, yarns, frames, and punch needle tools to complete basic patterns.

Step Five: Finish with Style

You just produced your first few patterns! It's time to display them on your favorite wall. Although there are lots of ways to finish your projects, we will simply frame them by gluing the fabric onto a straightforward wooden frame. Focus on the basic steps and leave the rest for the upcoming chapters. As you go through the different patterns in the book, you will find interesting ways to finish your projects, such as making a stool cover, using stuffing to make a stand-alone animal, using fabric glue to secure stitches, and many more techniques to achieve professionally crafted pieces of work.

Chapter Six:
Crafting Comfortable Pillows

Punch needle projects can easily be turned into comfortable and appealing pillows. Because punch needle embroidery is so sturdy, these pillows don't have to only be decorative. You can make your own everyday pillows that exactly match your decor and taste. This project can be made easier if you have a sewing machine, as hand sewing the two halves of the pillow can be time-consuming. If you're less worried about the pillow's durability, you can also use fabric tape or other options that replace sewing.

The punch needle project is great for a holiday-themed pillow. The pattern of Santa's face might seem more complicated than the house in the first project, but it's only adding one new idea. Instead of filling empty space with stitches, this task is going to help you practice using a single line of stitches to outline and add highlights to the embroidery. You can also go back and add the same sort of outlining to the house in the previous project. Adding this kind of outline can better define shapes and gives the whole project a crisper look. A single line can also be used to add elements to the image, such as the bobble on Santa's hat.

To get started, make sure you have all your materials ready to go. You'll need:

- A Punch needle

- Foundation fabric (such as monk's or weaver's cloth)

- Yarn, including black, white, and red colors

- An embroidery hoop

- Pattern - found on the next page

- Washable fabric marker or other marking tool

- Scissors

In order to turn this project into a pillow, you're going to need to take it out of the hoop. That means you don't want to glue the foundation fabric to keep it from slipping. You can use a bias band to make the hoop tighten a little more securely on the foundation fabric. Also, you'll use the excess foundation fabric as part of the pillow. Don't trim any off the edges, so that you'll have plenty later. If it gets in the way, you can pin it back.

Once you have all your materials, it's time to start. Note that many of the steps for this project are similar, if not that same, as the previous project. As a result, some steps might be covered in less detail.

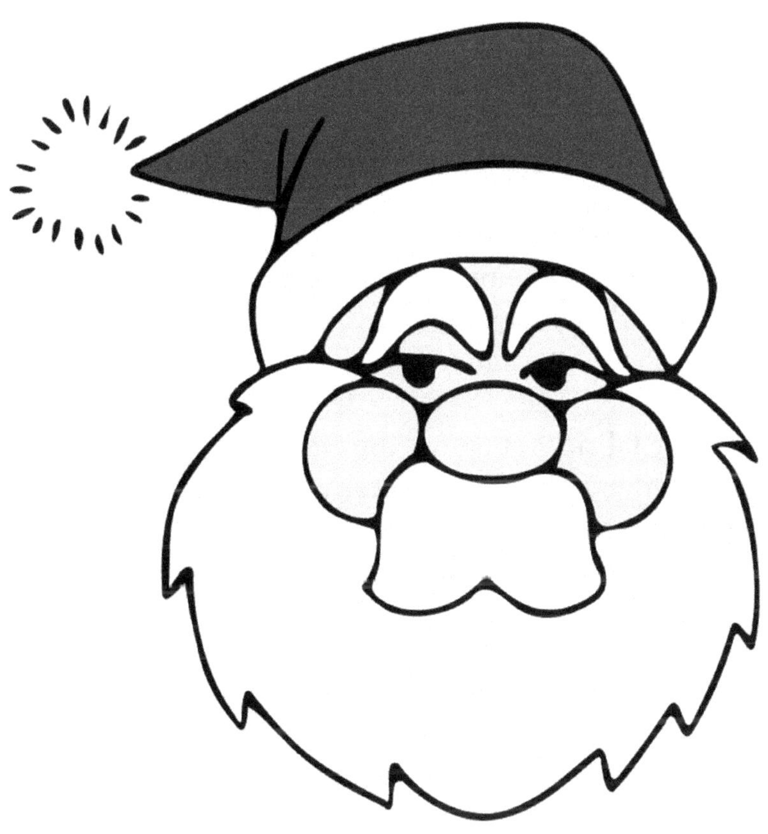

Step One: Transfer Your Pattern

Transferring the pattern to your foundation fabric doesn't really change, whatever the pattern or project you're working on. The same methods that we've already covered will work here as well, including a lightbox, carbon paper, or whatever method you've found works best for you.

When tracing this particular pattern, you might want to go over the black lines more than once to make them as wide and bold on the foundation fabric as they are on the pattern. Make sure that they're easy to follow.

Step Two: Prepare the Embroidery Hoop

It is probably wise to invest in a plastic embroidery hoop if you're planning on doing many projects, like this one, that are going to be taken out of the hoop to be finished. Alternatively, you can use the bias band trick again to keep the fabric from slipping too much. Pull the fabric taut across the embroidery hoop before you tighten it down completely. Again, remember that the tauter the fabric, the less effort you have to put into punching the needle through the fabric.

One thing to keep in mind with this project is that you're going to be filling the whole thing in with yarn stitches. Unless you want to leave some foundation fabric showing, that means the pillow you make can only be as big as the embroidery hoop you're using. That may be fine, particularly if you're following along to practice. If you want a larger pillow, you'll need to use a larger frame. If you don't want a round pillow, you can find square embroidery frames. In particular, there are heavier frames made for making rugs.

The other, cheaper, option is to make a square embroidery frame. This is a lot easier than it sounds and requires just a few materials. To make your own embroidery frame, you'll need:

- An artist's canvas (on a wooden frame).

- Foundation fabric.

- A flathead screwdriver and pliers (or something to remove staples).

- Either a stapler and staples or flat-headed tacks.

The wooden frame of the artist's canvas is going to turn into your embroidery frame. That means that the first thing you'll need to do is remove the canvas from the frame. Use the flathead screwdriver or pliers to remove the staples from around the edges of the frame. Note that the wooden frame may also be stapled together, and you *don't* want to remove *those* staples.

You can save the canvas for another project. Lay your foundation fabric out flat, and then lay the frame on top of it. Cut the foundation fabric to fit the frame, with about four inches of excess fabric. Stretch the fabric tightly across the frame and use staples to secure it. A normal office stapler obviously is not going to do the job. You'll want either a crafting stapler or a heavy-duty one you can find at a hardware store. Then again, you could gently hammer flat tacks in instead of using staples.

And you're all set. The fabric won't slip, as it would with a standard frame, as the foundation fabric is stapled down. Once you've finished the punch needle embroidery, you can pry the staples or flat tacks up once more. The holes shouldn't be visible, though, in the case of this project, that part of the fabric is going to end up hidden inside the pillow in any case.

Step Three: Prepare the Punch Needle

Use your threader to thread your punch needle, starting with black yarn. With punch needle embroidery, you always want to start on the outer edge of a design and work your way in. This prevents the loops and stitches from becoming sloppy as you go along and helps keep the shapes well defined. That means that, since you're outlining in black, you'll want to start with that color and go back and fill in the red and white.

With this project, you're much more likely to want the loop side showing, creating a fuzzy Santa face for your pillow. It will be important to make sure you're pushing the needle all the way to the stop with each stitch so that they are even.

Step Four: Start Punching

You've got everything you'll need and your fabric set up, so you might as well start punching. As mentioned before, it is a good idea to begin with the black outline first. Be sure to follow the technique that you practiced in the first project, turning the angular opening in the needle in the direction you're punching. The outline is only going to be one line wide, or perhaps second in some spots where you might go back over, for example, in the eyes. There are more corners and turns in this pattern than there were for the house, but it shouldn't affect how you punch at all. You're still just following the lines and turning the needle every time you reach a corner.

A lot of this project is going to end up being white, which means that your black outline is going to be important to give the image shape. When you're just doing one line, however, there's a tendency to rush through it and leave more room between stitches than you should. Be patient and keep the stitches even. You'll appreciate the time spent when you reach the end, and everything is neat and pretty.

Once you've finished outlining everything, you can move on to either the red or white yarn. Because this is a pillow, you'll probably want to fill in all the blank space with the white yarn so that your pillow looks finished and none of the foundation fabric is showing. That can be time-consuming, but it will make for a more comfortable pillow. In this case, you'll want to start at the edges and spiral in to fill the center. The edge, in this case, is just going to refer to the edge of the hoop. When the surface is filled in, you can remove the foundation fabric from the frame. At this point, it may not seem very flat, but don't worry. We'll fix that in the next step.

Step Five: Finish with Style

Turning Santa into a comfy pillow isn't going to take too much work. There are a few steps we want to take to make sure that this project isn't too frustrating, and you end up with an attractive end product. Before we get into that, though, let's review the materials for this second half of the project. Specifically, you'll need:

- Punch needle embroidery.

- Cotton backing fabric - red or green might work best with this holiday pillow.

- Stuffing for the pillow.

- Needle and thread in matching color.

- Pins.

- Scissors.

- Sewing machine or iron-on fabric tape (optional).

- Fray check.

- An iron and board.

- Washcloth or tea towel.

First, make sure that the cotton backing fabric is the same size as the punch needle embroidery. A little bit of variation is fine, as the edges are going to be folded under. It will make your life easier if the two pieces of cloth start out being the same shape, however.

There are a few steps to turning your punch needle embroidery into a pillow.

1. Steam your punch needle embroidery project. As you may have noticed when you removed the embroidery from the hoop so that the foundation fabric was no longer stretched tight, it is a little twisted and uneven. To fix this, get a thin towel, get it wet, then rinse it out so that it's wet but not sopping. Lay it over the punch needle embroidery, with the embroidery's loop side up. Preheat your iron (to a high temperature if using wool, a lower temperature if using polyester or a blend). Use the iron to press the fabric for a four-count. Pick the iron up and move it to press again. Don't slide the iron across the fabric. Be careful of the steam!

2. Once your embroidery has been steamed and allowed to dry, you can line it up with the cotton back fabric. Put them together so that the wrong side of both is on the outside. The loop side of the embroidery should be on the inside. In other words, the pillow should end up being inside out after you've sewn it. Match the two pieces of cloth and pin them together so that they can lay flat, one on the other.

3. Sew the two pieces together. *Leave an opening so you can stuff the pillow*. Again, remember the pillow should be inside out here. This is where a sewing machine comes in very handy.

You can hand sew the pillow together, but it will take a while, and the results probably won't be as even. An alternative is to use fabric tape or something similar, which will create the seam without any sewing. Those sorts of methods are usually much more durable. You can cut off any excess fabric at this point. Leave a little bit of material for the seam, though. At the seam, you can use fray check or some similar product to keep the edges from coming apart. It's important to remember this for the foundation fabric, in particular, as it can tend to fray.

4. Once you've got three edges sewn together, you can turn your pillow right side out. Punch needle embroidery is usually pretty durable, but you may want to do this reasonably gently. Taking care when flipping the pillowcase inside out means the loops are less likely to be disordered.

5. The pillow is almost done. Take the stuffing and begin shoving it into the pillow. It's difficult to put too much stuffing into a pillow. Once you think you've got it full, see if you can stuff another dozen handfuls in. The more filling, generally, the comfier the pillow!

6. Sew shut the opening. It is probably a good idea to pin it closed first to keep the stuffing in and make sewing it easier. Pull big wads of

stuffing into smaller pieces, as it will be easier
to even out the stuffing later. Use a ladder
stitch so that there are no rough edges sticking
out.

7. Punch that pillow! Basically, you're massaging
the stuffing a bit, so it's evenly distributed and
bunched in one corner.

You're all done! Project two is complete, and
you've got a comfy pillow all ready for Christmas.

Chapter Seven:
Punch a Fuzzy Friend

A fuzzy stuffed animal is a gift that is always treasured, no matter who receives it. That little fuzzy friend will mean all the more if it's something you put together with your own two hands. Needlepoint embroidery is a particularly great choice for making a stuffed animal, as the loop side is appropriately fuzzy.

Like the other projects in this book, it's simpler to do than you may think. It's going to be very similar to the project you just completed, making a pillow. As you may have guessed, however, we'll add one or two skills, both to keep things interesting and so you can add ideas to your punch needle embroidery bag of tricks. Using the stitches themselves, we're going to see a fairly simple trick for adding depth and texture to punch needle embroidery art.

To make a stuffed animal, you can sew a canvas or felt backing, as we did with the pillow. Another option is to punch needle embroider a second piece that can serve as a back side. With many stuffed animals, you can just fill in the back with a solid color of stitches. With this project, however, you can basically embroider the same pattern twice and then sew them together, so the stuffed animal has two finished sides. When prepping the second piece of embroidery, keep in mind that you want the looped right side to be on the outside for both halves. That means that the second piece should be mirrored. In other words, if the fish pattern is looking to the right for the first piece of embroidery, it should be facing to the left for the second. This will ensure that the two halves are 'facing the same way' and the looped side is facing outward, so your stuffed fish is properly fuzzy.

To get started, you'll need:

- A punch needle (and threading tool)

- Foundation cloth

- Yarn, at least 1 fill color and 1 outline color

- Embroidery hoop

- Pattern - found on the next page

- Washable fabric marker or other marking tool

- Scissors

- Bias band or other strips of thin cloth (optional)

- Glue (optional)

Remember, if you're going to be making two fishes to make into a complete piece, you'll need twice as much foundation fabric and yarn. There's some detail in the fish that you may also want to outline or highlight with a separate color of yarn. You can fill the fish in with one single color or choose to use a range of colors. There is enough variety in yarn colors that you could choose to do each scale in a different shade if you want to.

Weaver's cloth might be a good option for a foundation fabric, as it has a tighter weave that will do a better job of holding together. Though, you may want to use monk's cloth if you want a fuzzier buddy, as that would allow you to select a heavier yarn. Either way, be sure to use some method to keep the foundation cloth from fraying. Using a backing material like felt, instead of two pieces of embroidery back to back, will also help prevent fraying.

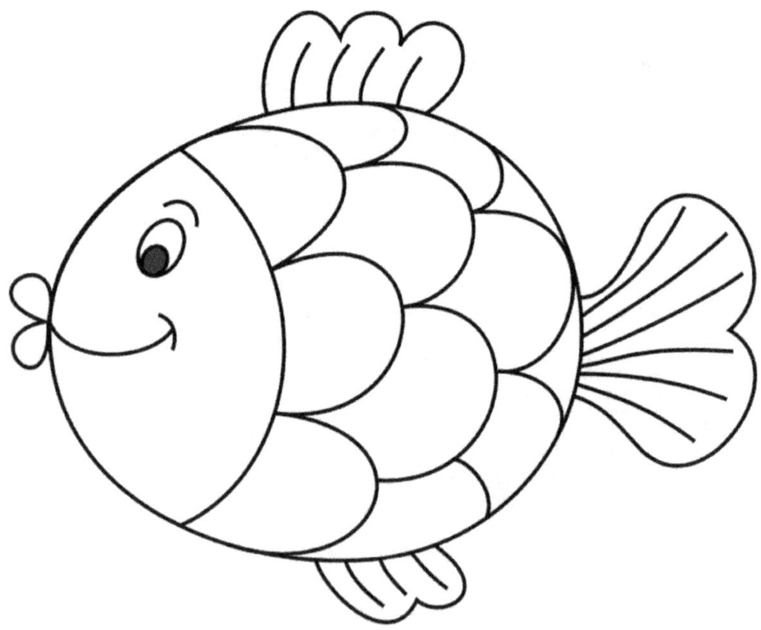

Step One: Transfer the Pattern

With the practice you've already had in transferring patterns, this step should be a snap! Lightboxes or carbon paper are both good methods, or you can use one you've found on your own. This pattern has more detail than the others that were used in previous projects, however; so don't get frustrated if it's a little fiddly.

Step Two: Prepare the Embroidery Hoop

Stretch your chosen foundation fabric across your embroidery hoop, then make sure the hoop is tightly secured. Remember, the tighter the foundation fabric is stretched in the embroidery hoop, the easier a time you'll have actually punching with the needle. However, *too* tight can lead to difficulties of another sort. Try to find that happy medium.

Again, since this project is destined to leave the embroidery hoop and go off on its own, you might want to make life easier on yourself and use a plastic embroidery hoop. They're easier to use, as they are easier to tighten and are better at preventing the fabric from moving. On the other hand, if you prefer to use a wooden hoop, wrapping the inner hoop in a bias band or another strip of fabric will help keep your foundation material in place.

Step Three: Prepare the Punch Needle

Using your punch needle threading tool, pass the first color yarn you're using through the needle. Again, starting from the outside and working your way in is the best way to go, so begin with the color you've chosen for outlining. Black is always a go-to favorite for creating an outline, even if you're going for a more colorful fish.

Step Four: Start Punching

Begin with the outline, tracing each line and fine. There are more lines on this project than the others we've done so far, so this might take a little longer to complete than with the other projects. It may be tempting to put stitches close together when outlining curves. Remember that putting stitches too close together can weaken the fabric. More importantly, it can lead to the fabric puckering after it is removed from the embroidery hoop, just like stretching the fabric too far. If you do find your fabric puckering, as we've already mentioned, steaming can help it lie flat.

Once you've finished the outline of the fish, scales, and fins, you can start filling in each section. Again, spiral into the center of each area, keeping the point of the needle near to the fabric. Try to stagger the stitches, so they don't line up.

As an alternative idea, you don't have to outline all the scales on the inside of the fish. Instead, use the way you stitch to give the scales shape. This is particularly effective if you mix up the color choices for the scales. All you have to do is punch your stitches along the curved side of the scale. Continue working your way in arcs toward the front of the fish, so that the stitches themselves are giving the scales shape. You can use a similar idea to give the impression of petals on a flower or to give the impression of brush bristles, both of which you'll be able to give a try with the projects you'll find later in the book. That's a subtle touch that you can try or not. Either way, you'll end up with a happy fish buddy.

Once you've filled in the whole interior of the fish, you're finished. You can take the fish out of the frame and put it aside. At this point, you can either decide to just back the fish with a simple, plain piece of felt. That's a slightly easier version and can be a good option if you're ready to put the punch needle aside for the moment or if you're excited to move on to a new project.

On the other hand, you can decide to make a completely fuzzy stuffed animal. To do that, you'll want to go through and repeat all the steps we've covered so far, one through three.

Just note, once more, that if you're using a second punch needle fish for your stuffed animal, you'll want to flip the second fish you do. That way, the loopy, right side will be facing out on both sides of the fish. Once you're ready, you can move on to finishing your project.

Step Five: Finish With Style

Turning your fish into a stuffed animal will require a little more work. As with the pillow, a sewing machine is going to be a real time-saver with this project. If you don't have access to one, you can embark on the project of hand sewing it all together, or you can go for fabric tape. Just note that the tape is going to be a less secure way of putting the project together.

As a potentially helpful hint, many libraries and community centers offer sewing machines for use on their premises or even allow them to be checked out and taken home. Check in your area, and you may be surprised what's available. It is also sometimes possible to find old sewing machines for good deals at Goodwill, eBay, or any place you can find second-hand stuff. In many cases, older machines were heavier and sturdier, and therefore of higher quality than modern versions, so you may end up with a great sewing machine for a rock-bottom deal.

As always, the first step is to make sure you have all your materials to hand before starting. To make a stuffed animal, you'll need:

- Your finished punch needle embroidery project(s)

- Backing material if you're not using a second piece of embroidery

- Needle and thread in a matching color

- Sewing machine or iron-on fabric tape

- Scissors

- Stuffing

- Pins

- Scissors

- Sewing machine or iron-on fabric tape (optional)

- Fray check

- An iron and board

- Washcloth or tea towel

1. As with the pillow, the first step you take should be to iron the embroidery piece so that it will lie flat and won't be bunched up around the stitches. Take a washcloth or tea towel and wet it thoroughly. Wring it out so that it is pretty wet but not dripping. Lay the embroidery flat on an ironing board, then lay the towel over the embroidery. Take your hot iron and press down firmly. Don't move the iron over the surface of the embroidery. Instead, lift it and move it before pressing down once more.

2. Once the embroidery has been flattened, you can trim off the excess foundation fabric around the fish. Leave about an inch of extra fabric around the edges. If you're using a backing material, lay the embroidery on top of it and trace the shape, then cut it out.

3. Pin the two halves of the stuffed animal together. Remember that you want the 'wrong' flat stitch side facing out, as you're going to turn everything inside out before stuffing it. Once everything is pinned together and lined up, you can begin to sew the two halves together. Leave a gap so that you'll be able to stuff it.

4. The animal has begun to take shape, and you may be getting an idea of how fabulous a fuzzy fish friend you're fabricating. Now, you just need to add the stuffing. As with the pillow, you'll probably want to stuff more in than you think you need. On the other hand, stuffed animals are usually not as full as pillows, so don't go too overboard. Pull big wads of stuffing apart into smaller bits.

5. Gently turn the whole thing inside out so that the loopy side is outside (on both sides). As with the pillow, you may need to take a moment to push the loops back in the right spot and clean everything up, as spending some

time inside out probably messed them up a bit. Using a ladder stitch, sew closed the gap.

6. Massage the stuffing so that it's evenly distributed.

You now have a little fishy friend to love or gift!

Chapter Eight:
An Art Stool

Crafting projects are great for adding a little beauty and appeal to your home, but the best crafting projects are also practical. With this project, you're both adding some color and charm to a stool top, while also making it a little more comfy by crafting a cover. Obviously, this project is going to be the most useful if you already have a stool to work with and one you want to cover. However, the cover can be adapted to other uses as well. It could be used as a little bag or to cover something else.

This is another project where you're probably going to want to fill all of the foundation fabric in the embroidery hoop with stitches. The stool top is going to be much more comfortable if you're sitting on a completely fuzzy seat. This might take a little longer, but the project overall should be less time consuming than some of the others in this book.

The pattern that comes with this project has more elements than the other projects we've worked on so far. However, they are primarily straight lines and so should be fairly easy to work with. This pattern also offers an opportunity to use an artistic technique in your punch needle embroidery. The brush and paint jar have a little bit of a reflection on them, which can make them appear somewhat three-dimensional. This is pretty easy to replicate in punch needle embroidery, just needing two shades of the same color, one somewhat lighter than the other. This technique works particularly well if you're planning on displaying the flat stitch side of your project rather than the loop side. On the other hand, you can simply fill in everything in a single shade and not worry about it.

To get started, you'll need:

- A punch needle (and threading tool)

- Foundation cloth

- Yarn, at least four colors, including a background color

- Embroidery hoop - Check the size of the stool top

- Pattern - found on the next page

- Washable fabric marker or other marking tool

- Scissors

- Bias band or other strips of thin cloth (optional)

- Glue (optional)

Step One: Transfer the Pattern

Use one of the methods detailed earlier in the book to transfer the pattern to your foundation fabric. If you don't want to bother with the lighter shade of yarn, you don't have to transfer those aspects of the pattern to the foundation fabric.

Step Two: Prepare the Embroidery Hoop

Before you stretch your foundation fabric in the embroidery hoop, take a moment to measure the top of the stool (or other object) you wish to cover. Embroidery hoops come in sizes from about a tiny 3 inches to about 14 inches. Ideally, the embroidery will cover the entire top face of the stool, so you'll want to use an embroidery hoop at least that wide, or even a little wider. Larger hoops are slightly more expensive but still shouldn't break the bank.

As in the other projects, lay the foundation fabric over the inner hoop, then place the outer hoop over the top. You can wrap the hoop in a bias band or other strips of fabric to keep the foundation fabric from slipping as you embroider. Remember to keep the fabric tight, but not too tight.

Step Three: Prepare the Punch Needle

Use your threading tool to prepare your punch needle with your first color of yarn. As before, you're going to start at the edges and spiral into the center to fill the entire space. That means you'll want to start with the outline color you've chosen.

Step Four: Start Punching

Start with the edges of each shape, working your way around the outside and then spiraling to the center. If you want to add the lighter colors to give some 3D depth to your project, don't outline the lighter sections in black. Doing so will ruin that effect to some extent. After this project, you will have a better appreciation for why punch needle embroidery is also called punch needle painting.

There's also a little space to experiment with another new idea. You can stitch the tip of the paintbrush in such a way as to give the impression of bristles. This method is only going to work if you're planning to display the flat stitch side. This method breaks one of the cardinal rules of punch needle embroidery, and, because of that, the loopy side will not look right.

The basic technique that you've been using so far keeps the stitches short, with the distance between the stitches being about the same as the diameter of the yarn. You can make longer stitches, however, which ends up looking a little different. In this project, you can use each long stitch as a bristle of the brush, from the handle to the tip or to where the color changes. Using a single long stitch, particularly if you use a dark brown color for the bristles, can give the embroidery a bit more texture.

For other projects, you can use this technique in other ways. It's become a popular way for rendering leaves, for example, using a darker and lighter shade of green to give a leaf some depth. In this next project, you can try that out for yourself, if you want. There are any number of other creative uses for a longer stitch.

The longer stitch isn't traditionally used in punch needle embroidery and tends to show up more in modern crafting projects. In the past, crafters were at least as concerned with durability as they were with appearance and the longer stitch is weaker. It leaves a length of yarn that can rub against the foundation fabric and fray or even be pulled away. It's also easy for the yarn to be displaced so that the foundation fabric can be seen underneath. The longer stitch is, therefore, probably best saved for projects that are primarily going to be decorative. If you want to make something that is hard-wearing, follow the traditional practice of keeping stitches smaller.

Since this pattern is destined to be a stool top, you'll probably want to cover the whole surface with yarn stitching, not leaving any bare foundation fabric. It's a little time consuming, but it will make for a more comfortable seat.

Once you've completed the embroidery, you can remove the piece of work from the hoop.

Step Five: Finish With Style

You'll need to do just one or two more things to turn your embroidery into a stool cover. There are just one or two things you need to finish. To make sure the cover fits the stool top snugly, you're also going to be adding a drawstring, covered in step-by-step directions. With the drawstring, you'll be able to tighten the cover down to the stool.

To finish your stool cover, you'll need:

- Your finished punch needle embroidery project

- Backing material

- Needle and thread in a matching color

- Sewing machine or iron-on fabric tape

- Scissors

- Cord for a drawstring

- Pins

- Scissors

- Sewing machine or iron-on fabric tape (optional)

- Fray check

- An iron and board

- Washcloth or tea towel

1. Following the example of the other projects, the first step is to steam the embroidery to be sure that it's flat. Wet your towel thoroughly and wring it out, so it's not dripping. Layer the embroidery and towel on your ironing board. Heat your iron to a temperature appropriate for the material. Using the same method as before, press the hot iron down firmly. Don't rub the iron across the towel. Instead, pick it completely up and then press it down once more.

2. The excess foundation fabric can be trimmed off once the embroidery has been flattened. For this project, you'll want to trim fairly close to the embroidery while still leaving a little bit of a fringe. This is going to be folded underneath to make a clean edge.

3. Take your backing material and lay it flat. Cut out a circle about 6 ½ inches wider across than your embroidery. This extra fabric is going to wrap around the stool top and hold the embroidery against the seat. You're also going to fold over part of it to make a casing for your drawstring.

4. Center the embroidery on the circle of backing material. As always, use some pins to keep the embroidery in place as you're working. The process of centering the embroidery on the backing material can be a bit of a pain. Marking

the center of each part on the wrong side can be helpful. Then pin the centers to each other. Lay them out, so they are flat, then pin around the edges.

5. Sew the punch needle embroidery to the backing material around the edge. Sewing by hand is always an option, though using a sewing machine is much faster. If you don't have a sewing machine or access to one, you may be able to find one available for use in your community center.

6. Next, you're going to add the drawstring around the edge of the backing material. Fold over the edge of the material. The drawstring is going to pass through this fold once it's sewn close, so it needs to be wide enough for the cord, plus about ¼ inch extra so the cord can pass easily. Remember to fold the edge of the fabric under so there are no raw edges showing.

7. Before you sew the casing closed, however, you want to make two holes for the drawstring to pass through the fabric casing to where it can be pulled tight and tied. There are a couple of ways to do this. One is to make two buttonholes in the casing. This is going to be most easily done using a sewing machine, but it can also be done by hand. Sewing a buttonhole is a useful skill, but it is also a bit of a process. There are plenty of tutorials online that can help you add

buttonholes to a project. You could also buy small grommets or other products that are available instead of sewing buttonholes.

8. Once you've got a couple of holes, you can sew the casing to the backing material. Remember to pin everything in the right place first, which will make sewing it much more manageable.

9. Using a thread and a safety pin, you can feed the cord through the drawstring casing. Tie stopper knots in the end of the casing to keep them from pulling back through.

All done! Take a moment to sit down and enjoy your much more comfortable and attractive stool.

Chapter Nine: Making A Patch

Punch needle embroidery is an incredibly versatile way of crafting attractive and fun decorations. This next project will allow you to take your embroidery and really put it just about anywhere. With some iron-on adhesive, it's simple to make a piece of punch needle embroidery into a patch. If sewing is something you have trouble with, then making a patch out of your embroidery project lets you put your own designs wherever you want. There is a small amount of sewing in this project, but it shouldn't be hard.

Patches are usually little expressions of your personality, a sort of concrete way of wearing your heart on your sleeve. Rather than working from a pattern on this project, you're going to draw something for yourself instead. Take a little bit of time and think about what you want to draw. It doesn't have to be complicated or a great work of art. A happy face works, or you can go looking online for some inspiration. Once you have an idea of what your design is going to be, you can jump into crafting.

To get started, you'll need:

- A Punch needle (and threading tool).

- Foundation cloth.

- Yarn.

- Embroidery hoop - Check the size of the stool top.

- Washable fabric marker or other marking tool.

- Scissors.

- Iron-on adhesive.

- Bias band or other strips of thin cloth (optional).

- Glue (optional).

Step One: Draw the Pattern

Instead of transferring the pattern, you now have the freedom to draw whatever you want. Freehanding a drawing is not a terrible idea if you're confident enough for that. You can also use stencils, rulers, or whatever shapes you have around. All that is important is that you think it looks good. Keep in mind what you've done so far as you've practiced punch needle embroidery. Start with shapes that you can fill in with color. Add an outline or highlights. It's probably best to keep the patch small and simple. It makes crafting it easier. Patches, in general, tend to be simple. Also, a simple design is better for a smaller piece. Straightforward designs are easier to see and understand from a distance.

Step Two: Prepare the Embroidery Hoop

Lay the inner hoop down on a flat work surface. Draw the pattern you've created over it, then secure the outer hoop around the foundation fabric. Pull the fabric so that it is tight across the inside of the hoop, but not drum tight. As before, a bias band can be used to create a tighter fit around the hoop if you're using a wooden hoop.

Step Three: Prepare the Punch Needle

Using a threading tool, thread your punch needle with the first color of yarn you're going to use. As always, you'll want to begin on the outside and work your in, so start with the appropriate color.

Step Four: Start Punching

With your design, you're in the driver's seat. Again, remember that you want to start at the outside of each shape and work your way in. Try to keep the needle at a right angle to the fabric so that it will flip through the weave as easily as possible. When punching around the outside of stitches you've already made, angle the needle slightly inward toward them. Spiral around the inside of shapes until everything is completely filled. Don't worry if there are a few sparse spots. There's nothing wrong with going back and adding a stitch or two if you need to. Punch needle embroidery is very forgiving of needing to fix mistakes.

Remember to keep your foundation fabric tight. It's worth it to take a few moments to pull it tight once more if it loosens. Keep the opening in the needle facing the direction you're moving the needle, turning the opening when you hit a corner or are changing directions. With this project, you'll probably want to stick with shorter stitches, each only about as long as the width of the yarn. Longer stitches, while they can give a nice effect and look appealing, are definitely less sturdy. For something like a patch, which is likely going to be worn on clothing or stuck on a bag, durability is something to keep in mind.

Once you've finished punching, you're ready to turn your design into a patch.

Step Five: Finish with Style

You'll need just a few more things to turn your punch needle embroidery into a patch. These supplies should be available in any hobby shop, though probably not with the fabric and thread.

To finish this project, you'll need:

- A needle and thread

- Iron-on adhesive

- Fray check

- A peel and stick film

- Sharp fabric scissors

Having finished punching your design, you can take it out of the embroidery hoop. Once you've got all your supplies, you can start turning your punch needle embroidery project into a patch.

1. Before you cut out the design, it's a good idea to cover one side with an iron-on adhesive. Since patches are worn on clothing and tend to be treated fairly roughly, adding the adhesive backing will keep all the stitches where they are supposed to be. Otherwise, you could end up with a patch that's going bald. To be clear, this iron-on adhesive is different from the peel and stick film and is made particularly for fabric projects. Alternatively, you can use a thin layer of fabric glue.

2. Once the adhesive has been applied, you can go ahead and cut out your design. Before you do anything else, use some fray check or fabric glue to keep the edges of the patch from fraying. Just a little bit to seal the edge of the fabric is all you should need.

3. To make doubly sure that the patch doesn't fray, and to add a nice border, you're going to sew around the edges of the patch. Thread a needle and put a stopper knot in the other end of the thread. Start at the back of the patch, right at the edge, and push the needle through. Pull the thread all the way through until you

run up against the stopper knot. Again, push the needle in through the back and pull it out the front of the patch. The stitches should be as tight as you can make them. The idea is to sew the two parts of the patch together. It's a little time-consuming, but it will lengthen the life of your patch a great deal.

4. Once you've got the edges of the patch sewn all the way around the edge, you can apply the peel and stick film to the back of the patch. Cut carefully around the edge of the patch to remove the excess sticky film.

You've now got a patch ready to go. Just peel off the back and stick it somewhere.

Chapter Ten:
Denim Design

Up until now, the projects have all used the traditional method of using monk's or weaver's cloth as a foundation fabric. That's just one way that punch needle embroidery can be used. As was mentioned in the introduction, punch needle embroidery has been used throughout its history to embellish clothing and decoration such as gowns or religious garments. As it happens, one of the most common fabrics in use today, denim, is also a decent option for a foundation fabric. Put these two facts together, and it's clear that punch needle embroidery can add a little decoration to a pair of jeans.

For your first denim punching project, it might be best to start with an older pair of jeans that you're not as worried about. This is definitely something you can do to embellish your favorite pair of jeans, but denim may not be as forgiving of mistakes as monk's or weaver's cloth. Using second-hand or thrift shop jeans can be a great option; punch needle embroidery is a great way to bring new life to older clothes. Find a $5 pair of jeans at your local second-hand shop and make them your own. Just be sure to check out the materials tag on the jeans. Remember that synthetics or synthetic blends are going to be more likely to stretch and will be tricky to use for punch needle embroidery. Keep an eye out for 100% cotton denim jeans, as they are going to work best.

To start this project, you'll need to gather together your usual punch needle embroidery materials. These include:

- Punch needle

- Embroidery hoop

- Yarn

- 100% cotton jeans

- Washable Marker

- Fabric glue

Note; you won't need any sort of foundation fabric, as we're using the denim jeans for that purpose.

Step One: Design the Pattern

For this project, you're going to be putting the pattern directly on jeans. This is a similar idea to a patch, just a little more permanent, so it's up to you what you want to draw. There are a host of free patterns available on the internet. Or, you could draw a heart or smiley face. Choose something that makes you happy. You may want to start small when adding embellishments to clothes, so it might be a good idea to keep your drawing no larger than a few inches.

As with other punch needle projects, you can display either the looped or flat stitched sides. With most projects, you can decide which you want to use at any point, but this one will require a little more planning. If you want the loopy side to be on the outside at the end, you'll need to turn the jeans inside out and draw your design on the inside. If you'd rather the flat stitch side shows, then draw your design on the outside of the jeans.

Step Two: Prepare the Embroidery Hoop

Make sure you have an embroidery hoop the correct size for your project. A small design will be easier with a smaller hoop. Also, a smaller hoop will be easier to use with a pair of jeans. Denim jeans are usually thicker material, so there probably isn't going to be a need for bias bands or fabric strips to keep the hoop tight.

Place the section of fabric with the design over the smaller, inside hoop. Fix and tighten the larger, outside hoop over the top. Pull the fabric tight around the edges, then tighten the hoop once more to keep everything in place. You might have to pull the fabric a little harder to tighten it properly.

Step Three: Prepare the Punch Needle

Use the threading tool to thread the punch needle with the first color of yarn you're using. Insert the tool down the length of the needle from the sharp point to the blunt end. Put the yarn through the wire loop, then pull the tool back through the needle. Insert the tool once more, this time through the hole in the point of the needle. Put the yarn through the loop and pull the tool back through once more.

Step Four: Start Punching

Start at the edges, outlining shapes. Fill the shapes in by spiraling into the center. Denim is probably the thickest foundation fabric you'll work with in the projects in this book. It might take a little more 'oomph' to get the needle through the weave of the jeans. Keep the opening of the needle pointing in the direction you're moving. Keep the needle close to the fabric and try to keep the stitches small. As with the patches, it's reasonable to expect the jeans are going to experience wear, so it's better if the embroidery is hard-wearing.

Don't be afraid to go back over bald spots. Check the 'right' side, the side that is going to be visible, every so often so you know if you need to go back over areas. Once you've finished punching in the design, you only need to do one more thing to finish.

Step Five: Finish with Style

To finish this project, you only need one thing:

- Fabric glue (washing machine safe)

The back of your punch needle embroidery should be secured, so the stitches don't pull out. This can be a particular problem with clothing, as you'll wear them sitting and standing, twisting or bending over, all the while stretching the fabric of your jeans. That can quickly lead to lost stitches.

To stop that happening, coat the wrong side of the embroidery with a thin layer of glue so that it all holds together. Glue is preferable to the iron-on adhesive used in other projects since you're probably going to want to wash your jeans eventually. You could hand-wash them, but using some washing machine safe fabric glue is probably easier.

You now have some beautifully decorated jeans! Keep in mind that denim is only one of the possible options for punch needle embroidery foundation fabrics. You can also do this in a pure cotton shirt or sweater if you want.

Chapter Eleven:
Do-It-Yourself Punch Needle and Threader

If you're looking for a challenge, you may want to try making your own punch needle. Punch needles are usually not that expensive, and you can find them in kits with the whole kit costing no more than US$10. However, making your own punch needle is a fun little project, and, at the end, you'll have a punch needle customized to exactly what you like. The punch needles you buy are designed to be comfortable and easy to use, but everything can always be improved.

With this project, you're going to get your hands a little dirty. Instead of working with thread and needle, you're going to need a file, a hammer, and pliers. A pair of work gloves, while not strictly required, might save some wear and tear on your hands. It is also important to wear eye protection when using tools and particularly when working with wire. Additionally, you can use found or upcycled materials in this project, rather than buying what you need. Just be sure everything is cleaned and safe before starting the project.

To make your punch needle, you'll need:

- A pair of pliers/wire cutters.

- Copper wire of two different sizes.

- Metal, hollow umbrella rod.

- A nail of suitable size.

- A hammer.

- A flat file.

- A saw with metal cutting blade.

- A small ring.

The nails are going to be used to poke the hole in the tip of the needle. That means you'll need a nail that is 1) a little wider than the widest yarn you're hoping to use, and 2) not so wide you risk breaking the nail. The two wires can either be coated or stripped, as they'll be used to make the grip. Stripped wires might be a little easier to work with. Coated wires will mean that the grip of the punch needle will be coated.

The umbrella rod you're going to use is the hollow rods that form the ribs of a regular umbrella. These are usually hollow, so they are lighter but still fairly strong, and they make for a great base for a punch needle. The easiest place to find this is, obviously, in an old umbrella. Don't take your roommates apart, but if you happen to have one you don't need lying around, you can find some hugely useful materials by dismantling it. Thrift and second-hand shops are also excellent places to find old umbrellas at a real deal.

Take a moment to prepare all your materials. Make sure all the metal is clean and ready to go. Once everything is ready, you can jump into the project.

Step One: Cut and Shape Umbrella Rod

The umbrella rod is going to form the basis of the punch needle, so we need to start with roughing out a general shape for the needle. Decide how long your needle needs to be. It should be long enough to fit in your hand, plus a few extra inches. It shouldn't be so long that it's hard to manage, however. Measure out a length of umbrella rod (measure twice, cut once!). Use your saw with a metal cutting blade to cut the umbrella rod to the length you've determined. It can help to secure the rod in a vise to keep it stable. If you don't have a vise, brace the rod on the edge of a table, with the part of the rod you're discarding projecting beyond the edge. Start the cut by drawing the blade toward you once or twice to create a little divot to rest the edge of the saw in. The rod should be cut in only a few strokes. Take your file and run it over the cut edge to remove any burrs.

Next, you'll need to cut the rod diagonally across. This will create a point for the needle. It's pretty tough to start a saw cutting at an angle, particularly on a smooth, hollow rod. You'll need to start the cut again, cutting at right angles to the rod to make that small divot hold the saw's edge. Then, you can start to cut at an angle to create the point of the needle. Take your time and be patient. The rod should cut fairly quickly if you don't rush the job.

Once the angle has been cut, take your file and once more smooth everything out. It's important that there not be any rough or sharp spots. Nor should there be any hard corners. This all needs to slip easily between the weave of the foundation fabric, so any place where a thread can catch is going to make that more difficult. Worse, a sharp metal burr can damage or cut thread or yarn. You're going to be running the file over the whole thing several more times through the process, but taking the time to smooth things out as you go will save you time later. Metal burrs and rough spots can also damage *you*, which is a good way to ruin your crafting fun.

Step Two: Punch a hole in the Needle

If you've done some of the projects in this book already, you'll have some idea of how a punch needle is supposed to work. One important part of the needle is the hole in the point, which will 'carry' the yarn back and forth through the foundation fabric.

To add this hole, you'll need a nail (or metal punch) and a hammer. Choose a spot on your needle, near the point but not right at the tip, where you're going to put your hole. Its exact location isn't super vital, just so long as the yarn is carried closely behind the point of the needle.

Do your best to secure your umbrella rod, with the open side of the point facing up. If using a vice, be careful that you don't end up flattening the umbrella rod by over-tightening.

Place the point of the nail on your chosen spot. Keep it at right angles to the surface of the needle, straight up and down. Hit the head of the nail sharply with your hammer. One hit should probably be enough to make a hole, but you might need to take another whack or two to ensure that yarn can slip through without a problem. Take your file and once more smooth everything out as much as possible.

Step Three: Twist wire for the grip

You're making your own grip as the slippery metal of the umbrella rod is probably going to be difficult to push through the foundation fabric. It's going to be easier to do that with a fatter grip that we can hang on to tightly. To make something comfortable, you're going to twist those two lengths of wire together. Twisted wire grips are easy to put together and actually quite traditional.

To do this, you'll need to start by taking the thinner wire that you've chosen and measuring out enough wire for the grip. You'll need to estimate, which you can do by wrapping the thin wire around the umbrella rod, leaving a little bit of space between the wraps. Leave some extra space. You're going to need to stretch this out fairly tautly, so it should be wrapped or tied to something and then pulled out straight. If you don't have anything else, you can use the claw size of the hammer as a hook and have a friend hold the hammer still.

Take the thicker wire, and, keeping it straight and taut, begin wrapping the thicker wire around the thinner wire. The loops should be quite tight to the thinner wire. They should also be fairly close together. The more tension you can keep in the thinner, backbone wire, the easier it will be to wrap. Leave a little bit of the thinner wire bare at either end. Once you've wrapped enough to cover the grip, you can clip off the excess wire. You can take a flat file and round off the ends of the wires, so they're not sharp, then bend them down as much as possible.

Step Four: Wind the Wire Grip

Take the thinner wire at the end of the grip wrap, and wrap it several times around the shaft of the umbrella rod tightly, between one and two inches from the sharp point of the needle. This is going to be the stop, where the punch needle runs up against the foundation fabric. Wrap the wire over and around itself as tightly as possible. You can then wrap the rest of the grip around the shaft of the needle. Again, keep the wire as tight as possible. This will keep the grip secure and fix it more securely to the needle.

The thicker wire that has been wrapped in loops will fan apart, creating a textured grip that will be easy to hold on to. Wrap the bare thin wire around the butt end of the needle. Before you secure everything, take a moment, and tighten your hand around the grip and test how tightly it is wrapped. If it seems loose or shifts, it's worth taking the time to tighten it up. A little more effort now will save frustration later.

Take the very end of the wire and pass it under itself, around the needle. Use your pliers to pull the wire tight into a knot, then trim it off. Round off the end of the wire and then bend it down.

Step Five: Shape and File the Needle

You've just about finished making your personal DIY punch needle. The last step is to take a hammer and examine the needle and grip. It might be a good idea to flatten or shape the point of the needle so that it will slip more easily into the weave of the foundation fabric. Make any other adjustments you'd like. Run a file over everything a final time, paying particular attention to the point of the needle. Once it's smoothed to your satisfaction, you're all done.

Step Six: Punch Needle Threader

It might almost be more useful to know how to make a threader than the punch needle itself. Most, if not all, of the punch needles you can buy, will come with a threader. The only notable exception is the Oxford punch needle, as it's designed with a slot down the whole length, rather than being hollow.

You may find that the threader that came with your punch needle quickly disappears, though, unless you're an especially organized crafter. It's essentially just a thin piece of wire, and it's easy to imagine it being misplaced, overlooked, or used for some other purpose and forgotten about. Unfortunately, threading a punch needle without one can be tremendously aggravating. Rather than fiddling around with makeshift solutions, just take a few moments and craft a new threader that you can store with your punch needle. Repeat as necessary.

To make a threader, all you'll need is:

- Thin wire

- A small ring - the sort of ring you put your keys on is great

- A pair of pliers/wire cutters

Ideally, you used a reasonably stiff wire for the grip. The copper wire you find in craft stores for jewelry is a perfect option. For the threader, a thinner, more flexible wire will work better. Something like picture wire or piano wire will work well. You'll need a piece of wire three times as long as the total length of the punch needle you're making it for.

Measure and mark the halfway point on the wire. Fold it at that point, then crimp the fold with your pliers. That forms a little point that will be easy to put through the punch needle.

Take the ring and the two ends of the wire. Leaving about an inch-long tail of wire, wrap the two ends around the ring, together, over, and then back around. Use the pliers to keep the wrapping tight. To secure the ends, take your pliers and grip all the wires just below the ring. Twist the ring gently so that the wires twist around and secure themselves.

With a few tools and some elbow grease, you can make everything you need for punch needle embroidery, all by yourself.

Chapter Twelve: Homemade Embroidery Frame

For some projects, the store-bought frames that you'd regularly use just aren't going to cut it. You may need an odd size for a specific project, or maybe you have a brilliant idea that needs an odd shape, but there's nothing you can find in a crafting store. Crafting is all about tailoring your life to your needs, after all, which means that sometimes you're going to need to make your own tools.

You've already read about using the frames from artists' canvases to make your own embroidery frame, which can be a low cost and simple way to find a square or rectangular frame. You can go even further, though, and make a frame yourself from just a few pieces of wood, a few tools, and a little time. Making a punch needle was a snap. Making a punch needle embroidery frame isn't going to be much more difficult. There are one or two tricky bits, but there will be some detailed instructions on how to handle those areas.

To make your embroidery frame, you'll need:

- Wood for your frame, of your choice.

- A saw, or something to cut the wood with.

- Ruler or measuring tape.

- A miter-box, carpenter's square, or protractor.

- Wood glue.

- sandpaper.

- Staples, small nails, or tacks (optional).

You can find wood for your frame at a craft store or hardware store. It should be about 1 inch wide and at least 2 inches longer than your desired frame size. Check out the wood used for an artist's canvas to get an idea of what will work best.

Cutting the wood so that the corners meet evenly is one of the trickier things to do in basic carpentry. Carpenters call it a miter joint, with a specific tool designed to make cutting those sorts of joints easier. Most big-box hardware stores will have a cheap plastic version available that will work fine for this project. You can also sometimes find them at second-hand or thrift stores, particularly those specializing in old tools. If you don't have a miter box and can't get one, don't lose hope. There are a bunch of methods for making a miter joint come out right, a couple of which will be covered in this book. More can be found with a little research until you find one that works well for you.

Remember that safety is vital. Eye protection is always a great idea when cutting wood or using sharp tools. Work gloves are also a good idea.

Once you have all your materials and tools collected, you can get started.

Step One: Cut Your Wood to Length

If it isn't already cut correctly, measure, mark, and cut the wood to the lengths you'll need. The wood should be about 1 inch wide and about 2 inches longer than the width you need for the frame. For example, if you wanted to make a frame 6 inches square, all of the wood should be cut to 8 inches long. If you wanted a rectangular frame, for example, 6x8 inches, you would need two pieces 8 inches long and two pieces 10 inches long.

Step Two: Cut the Miter Joints

To make a clean, strong corner in the frame, all of the framing wood needs to be cut at a 45-degree angle. This is a little trickier than it seems since even a small mistake becomes very obvious when you go to put the corners together. Since carpenters need to make corners frequently, they've come up with a number of ways to make cutting miter joints simple. A few methods will be covered here. If you find yourself without the exact right tool, you can probably find a workaround online with a little looking.

One tip to remember: you want all the cuts facing the same way. That is, when you're done cutting a piece of wood, one side should be longer than the other. All the pieces will fit together that way.

Method 1: Miter Box

This is the easiest method, by far. A miter box is a tool that is two parts; the box itself and a square-ish looking wood saw that goes with it. The box has several openings in it along both sides. To use it, lay the wood in the box flat. Place the saw in opposing openings; you want a 45-degree angle, which will be indicated on the box. Then, all you have to do is saw through the wood. The measuring has already been taken care of. Do this for each piece, remembering you want both cuts to point to the same side.

Method 2: Carpenter's square, ruler, or measuring tape

If you don't have a miter box, the next method is still pretty easy. For this one, though, you'll have to do your own measuring.

First, measure one inch from the end of your wood. Mark there, then draw a line straight across. There's a couple of ways to do this. If you have a carpenter's square, you can line it up at your one inch mark and then draw a line across. Another method is to measure one inch on both sides, then draw a line from one measuring mark to the other. Draw a line from the one inch mark to the corner, marking out the cut for the corner. Do this on the other side as well, remembering that you want both cuts pointing toward the short side of the framing piece. Once you've marked the lines out, you can begin sawing.

This can be a bit tricky, and the saw may have a tendency to slide around so close to the end of the wood. Draw the saw toward you a few times to create a divot in the wood, which will 'start' the cut. You can then begin sawing, confident the saw won't jump around. Make the cuts on both sides of all four pieces of wood.

Method 3: Use a Protractor

Both of the other methods are much easier to use and should probably be the first things you try. The exception is when you want to make a corner that isn't a simple right angle. Making the cuts becomes more complicated at that point, and you'll need to measure out the precise angles for the joint to meet smoothly.

Step Three: Sand the Corners and Rough Edges

Take some sandpaper and take off the rough edges. This will make it easier to fit the frame together and make for a more finished final product.

This is an opportunity to check your work and see if your corner cuts line up. Don't be too disappointed if they don't on the first try. It's a skill that usually has to be practiced. If things didn't work out, though, you could now hide that fact a bit by sanding down the corners so that they meet a little more evenly. You don't want to go too crazy, or you might take off enough material that one side of the frame is shorter than the other.

Step Four: Glue and Press

Put a bit of glue on one side of a joint. Press them together and hold them firmly. You can even put the pieces in a vise to let the glue set if you want. It's a common mistake to put too much glue into a joint, as many people may assume that more glue equals a stronger joint. It's a natural assumption, but it's not really true. You want to use just enough glue to cover the faces of each joint, so that the two pieces have a chance to adhere to each other.

If you're worried the joints won't hold for some reason, or you prefer a sturdier frame, you can use staples, nails, or wood tacks. You don't want to use anything too big, as the wood is fairly narrow. A big nail will end up splitting the wood and ruining your work so far.

Step Five: Clean It Up

You've got your frame all made. All you have to do now is clean it up. Use sandpaper to take off the rough edges (and spots where the corners don't quite match). It's also possible some glue seeped out of the sides of the joint. You can sand it down or use turpentine or a chemical remover to take it off. You can use some turpentine to clean off any sawdust or dirt.

The frame should be finished and ready for use in your next punch needle embroidery project.

Chapter Thirteen:
Tips for Beginners

Needle punching is a very relaxing craft and opens up endless possibilities for those just beginning on their creative journey. To become a pro in no time, you want to follow basic advice for success:

- *Learn to pair your punch needle with the right foundation cloth* - This is a skill you want to learn over time. By following the advice throughout the book, you will gradually understand what works best. In general, you want to make sure the size of the punch needle matches the weaving in the fabric.

- *Choose the right yarn* – The other core aspect of needle punching is to choose a yarn that fits well with the punch needle of your choice. While a thin needle may require just three strands, a regular needle will most likely require a thicker yarn. Once you are through the rest of the chapters in the book, it's easy to understand how to make a prudent choice for your pattern.

- *Know the difference between rug hooking and needle punching* - As you start experimenting with different designs and look up similar projects online, you are likely to run into rug hooking as well. Although the final results can look similar, the two techniques are very different. It's also nice to know needle punching is far easier than rug hooking.

- *Don't worry about uneven loops* - With needle punching, you need not worry about uneven loops. You simply pull the yarn to undo the loops, smooth the surface of the fabric, and start punching again.

Final Words

Punch needle embroidery is a wonderfully simple way of crafting. You can learn how to do it in just a moment and quickly start creating your own unique art and projects. The truth is that punch needle embroidery is a bit like painting, in that you can just put color and shape where you want without having to worry too much about fancy technique or counting knots. As a result, it's an easy, fun, and intuitive way to craft terrific individual clothes and decor.

The simplicity of this craft has made it a popular art form for the several hundred years punch needle embroidery has been around. It was used, in a restrained and respectful way, to decorate the vestments of religious people, as well as the everyday clothing of ordinary folk. Refined artists in Japan practice the variation called banku, which is even closer to oil painting than other forms of punch needle embroidery. Today, it's becoming more and more popular as an easy and inexpensive way to decorate your home. Even more, these days, it's quick to pick up and is a great hobby to keep you busy. Each of these styles, and the people who practice them, are connected regardless of time or place. Each one can learn from the other. As you continue to practice punch needle embroidery, you should feel free to draw from all of the traditions when creating projects of your own.

Punch needle embroidery has been compared to painting several times in this book, but a more modern comparison might actually be coloring books. The patterns that a crafter might use are like the outlines in coloring books waiting to be filled in. Just as, when you were a kid, the decision on whether to stay in or out the lines was entirely up to you. While the patterns give you a starting point and an inspiration, you can always put your own touch of creativity or style on a project. Hopefully, in this book, you've learned how punch needle embroidery works, as well as some tips on how to make each project your own.